Best 10 Arduino Projects for future development

Copyright © Anbazhagan.k

Best 10 Arduino Projects for future development

Contents at a Glance   PageNo

Acknowledgments

The writer might want to recognize the diligent work of the article group in assembling this book. He might likewise want to recognize the diligent work of the Raspberry Pi Foundation and the Arduino bunch for assembling items and networks that help to make the Internet Of Things increasingly open to the overall population. Yahoo for the democratization of innovation!

Introduction

The Internet of Things (IOT) is a perplexing idea comprised of numerous PCs and numerous correspondence ways. Some IOT gadgets are associated with the Internet and some are most certainly not. Some IOT gadgets structure swarms that convey among themselves. Some are intended for a solitary reason, while some are increasingly universally useful PCs. This book is intended to demonstrate to you the IOT from the back to front. By structure IOT gadgets, the per user will comprehend the essential ideas and will almost certainly develop utilizing the rudiments to make his or her very own IOT applications. These included ventures will tell the per user the best way to assemble their very own IOT ventures and to develop the models appeared. The significance of Computer Security in IOT gadgets is additionally talked about and different systems for protecting the IOT from unapproved clients or programmers. The most significant takeaway from this book is in structure the tasks yourself.

1.Track A Vehicle on Google Maps using Arduino, ESP8266 & GPS

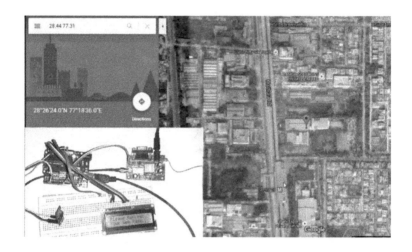

Vehicle Tracking System turns out to be significant now days, particularly in the event of stolen vehicles. On the off chance that you have GPS framework introduced in your vehicle, you can follow you Vehicle Location, and its causes police to follow the Stolen Vehicles. Already we have assembled comparable venture in which Location directions of Vehicle are sent on Cell Phone, check here 'Arduino based Vehicle Tracker utilizing GPS and GSM.

Here we are constructing further developed variant of Vehicle Tracking System at which you are able to Track your Vehicle on Google Maps. In this venture, we will send the area directions to the Local Server and you simply need to open a 'site page' on your PC or versatile, where you will discover a Link to Google Maps through your Vehicles Location Coordinates. When you click on that connect, it takes you on Google Maps, demonstrating your vehicles area. At this Vehicle Tracking System utilizing Google Maps, GPS Module is utilized for getting the area organizes wi fi module to keep send information to PC or portable over Wi-Fi and Arduino is utilized to make GPS and Wi-Fi converse with one another.

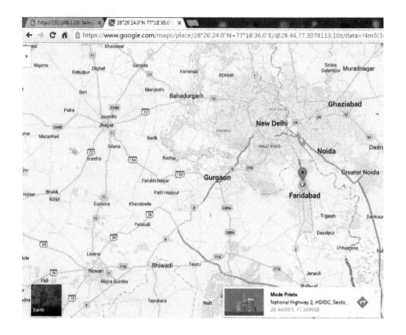

How it Works:

To follow the vehicle, we have to discover the Coordinates of Vehicle by utilizing GPS module. GPS module discusses constantly with the satellite for getting organizes. At that point we have to send these directions since GPS to Arduino by utilizing UART. And after that Arduino extricate the required information from got information by GPS.

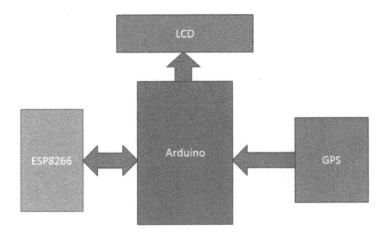

Prior to this, Arduino sends order to Wi-Fi Module ESP8266 for designing and associating with the switch and getting the IP address. After it Arduino introduce GPS for getting organizes and the LCD demonstrates a 'Page Refresh message'. That implies, client needs to invigorate website page. At the point when client invigorates the site page Arduino gets the GPS organizes and sends the equivalent to site page (nearby server) over Wi-Fi, with some extra data and a Google maps interface in it. Presently by clicking this connection client sidetracks to Google Maps with the organize and after that he/she will get the Vehicle Current Location at the Red spot on the Google Maps.

Components Required:

1. Arduino UNO
2. Connecting wires
3. Laptop
4. GPS module
5. Wi-Fi Module ESP8266
6. USB Cable
7. Bread Board
8. Power supply
9. Wi-Fi router
10. 16x2 LCD

Circuit Explanation:

Circuit for this 'Vehicle Tracking utilizing Google Maps venture' is straightforward and we for the most part need an Arduino UNO, GPS Module and ESP8266 Wi-Fi module. There is a 16x2 LCD alternatively associated for showing the status. This LCD is associated at 14-19 (A0-A5) Pins of Arduino.

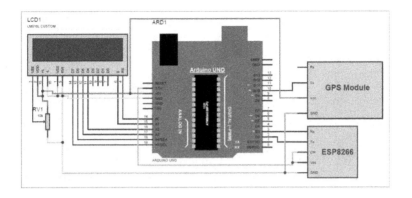

Here Tx stick of GPS module is straightforwardly associated with computerized stick number 10 of Arduino. By utilizing Software Serial Library here, we have permitted sequential correspondence on stick 10 and 11, and made them Rx and Tx individually and left the Rx stick of GPS Module open. Of course Pin 0 and 1 of Arduino are utilized for sequential correspondence however by utilizing SoftwareSerial library, we can permit sequential correspondence on other computerized pins of the Arduino. 12 Volt connector is utilized to control the GPS Module. Experience here to realize "How to Use GPS with Arduino" and get the directions.

Wi-Fi module ESP8266's Vcc and GND pins are legitimately associated with 3.3V and GND of Arduino and

CH_PD is likewise associated with 3.3V. Tx and Rx pins of ESP8266 are straightforwardly associated with stick 2 and 3 of Arduino. Programming Serial Library is likewise utilized here to permit sequential correspondence on stick 2 and 3 of Arduino. We have officially secured the Interfacing of ESP8266 Wi-Fi module to Arduino in detail, additionally please experience "How to Send Data from Arduino to Webpage utilizing WiFi" before doing this venture. The following is the image of ESP8266:

ESP8266 have two LEDs, first is Red, for showing Power as well as second is Blue for Data Communication LED. Blue LED flickers when ESP sends a few information through its Tx stick. Additionally, don't interface ESP to +5 volt supply generally your gadget may harm. Here in this task, we have chosen 9600 baud rate for all the UART interchanges.

Client can likewise observe the correspondence between Wi-Fi module ESP8266 and Arduino, on the Serial Monitor, at the baud pace of 9600:

GPS Degree Minute to Decimal Degree Conversion of Coordinates:

GPS Module gets facilitates from satellite in Degree Minute arrangement (ddmm.mmmm) and here we need Decimal Degree position for hunt the area on Google Maps. So first we have to change over directions from Degree Minute Format to Decimal Degree Format by utilizing given equation.

Assume 2856.3465 (ddmm.mmmm) is the Latitude that we get structure the GPS Module. Presently initial two numbers are Degrees and remaining are Minutes.

So 28 is degree and 56.3465 is minute.

Presently here, no compelling reason to change over Degree section (28), yet just need to change over Minute part into Decimal Degree by partitioning 60:

1. Degree organize = degree + minute/60

2. Decimal degree arrange = 28 + 0 94

3. Decimal degree facilitate = 28 + 56 3465/60

4. Decimal degree facilitate = 28 94

Same procedure will be accomplished for Longitude Data. We have changed over directions from Degree Minute to Decimal Degree by utilizing above formulae in Arduino Sketch:

```
float minut= lat_minut.toFloat();

minut=minut/60;

float degree=lat_degree.toFloat();

latitude=degree+minut;



minut= long_minut.toFloat();

minut=minut/60;

degree=long_degree.toFloat();
```

```
logitude=degree+minut;
```

Programming Explanation:

In this code, we have utilized SerialSoftware library to interface ESP8266 and GPS module with Arduino. At that point we have characterized various pins for both and introduce UART with 9600 baud rate. Likewise included LiquidCrystal Library for interface LCD with Arduino.

```
#include<SoftwareSerial.h>

SoftwareSerial Serial1(2,3); //make RX arduino line is pin 2
, make TX arduino line is pin 3.

SoftwareSerial gps(10,11);



#include<LiquidCrystal.h>

LiquidCrystal lcd(14,15,16,17,18,19);
```

After it, we have to characterize or proclaim variable and string for various reason.

```
String webpage="";

int i=0,k=0;

int gps_status=0;

String name="<p>1. Name: Your Name </p>";    //22

String dob="<p>2. DOB: 12 feb 1993</p>";     //21

String number="<p>4. Vehicle No.: RJ05 XY 4201</p>";//
29

String cordinat="<p>Coordinates:</p>";       //17

String latitude="";

String logitude="";

String gpsString="";

char *test="$GPGGA";
```

At that point we have made a few capacities for various purposes like:

Capacity for getting GPS information with directions:

```
void gpsEvent()



{

gpsString="";

while(1)

{

while (gps.available()>0)

{

char inChar = (char)gps.read();

gpsString+= inChar;

if (i < 7)

{
```

```
if(gpsString[i-1]  != test[i-1])

    {

    i=0;

    ..... ....

    ..... .....
```

Capacity for extricating information from GPS string and convert that information to decimal degree design from the decimal moment position, as clarified earliar.

```
void coordinate2dec()

{



    String lat_degree="";

    for(i=18;i<20;i++)

    lat_degree+=gpsString[i];
```

```
String lat_minut="";

for(i=20;i<28;i++)

  lat_minut+=gpsString[i];

    ..... ....

    ..... .....
```

Capacity for sending directions to ESP8266 for designing and associating it with WIFI.

```
void connect_wifi(String cmd, int t)

{

 int temp=0,i=0;

 while(1)

 {
```

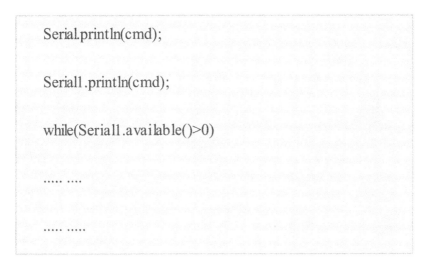

```
Serial.println(cmd);

Serial1.println(cmd);

while(Serial1.available()>0)

..... ....

..... .....
```

void show_coordinate() work for demonstrating coordinate on the LCD as well as Serial Monitor as well as void get_ip() work for getting IP address.

Void Send() work for making a String of data that will be sent to page utilizing ESP8266 and void sendwebdata() Function for sending data string to website page utilizing UART.

In void circle work Arduino consistently hang tight for solicitation structure site page (Refreshing website page).

```
void loop()
```

```
{

k=0;

Serial.println("Please  Refresh  Ur Page");

lcd.setCursor(0,0);

lcd.print("Please  Refresh  ");

lcd.setCursor(0,1);

lcd.print("Your  Web Page..  ");

while(k<1000)

..... ....

..... .....
```

Check the Full Code Below.

Code

#include<SoftwareSerial.h>

```
SoftwareSerial Serial1(2,3);    //make RX arduino line is pin
2, make TX arduino line is pin 3.

SoftwareSerial gps(10,11);

#include<LiquidCrystal.h>

LiquidCrystal lcd(14,15,16,17,18,19);

boolean No_IP=false;

String IP="";

String webpage="";

int i=0,k=0;

int gps_status=0;

String name="<p>1. Name: Your Name </p>";    //22

String dob="<p>2. DOB: 12 feb 1993</p>";    //21

String number="<p>4. Vehicle No.: RJ05 XY
4201</p>";//29

String cordinat="<p>Coordinates:</p>";    //17

String latitude="";

String logitude="";

String gpsString="";
```

```
char *test="$GPGGA";

void check4IP(int t1)

{

  int t2=millis();

  while(t2+t1>millis())

  {

    while(Serial1.available()>0)

    {

      if(Serial1.find("WIFI GOT IP"))

      {

        No_IP=true;

      }

    }

  }

}

void get_ip()

{

  IP="";
```

```
char ch=0;

while(1)

{

 Serial1.println("AT+CIFSR");

 while(Serial1.available()>0)

 {

  if(Serial1.find("STAIP,"))

  {

   delay(1000);

   Serial.print("IP  Address:");

   while(Serial1.available()>0)

   {

    ch=Serial1.read();

    if(ch=='+')

    break;

    IP+=ch;

   }

  }
```

```
  if(ch=='+')
   break;
  }
  if(ch=='+')
  break;
  delay(1000);
 }
lcd.clear();
lcd.print(IP);
lcd.setCursor(0,1);
lcd.print("Port:  80");
Serial.print(IP);
Serial.print("Port:");
Serial.println(80);
delay(1000);
}
void connect_wifi(String  cmd, int  t)
{
```

```
int temp=0,i=0;

while(1)

{

  Serial.println(cmd);

  Serial1.println(cmd);

  while(Serial1.available()>0)

  {

    if(Serial1.find("OK"))

    {

i=8;

    }

  }

  delay(t);

  if(i>5)

  break;

  i++;

}

if(i==8)
```

```
{

  Serial.println("OK");

}

else

{

Serial.println("Error");

}

  delay(1000);

}

void setup()

{

  Serial1.begin(9600);

  Serial.begin(9600);

  lcd.begin(16,2);

  lcd.print("Vehicle Tracking");

  lcd.setCursor(0,1);

  lcd.print("    System    ");

  delay(2000);
```

```
lcd.clear();

lcd.print("WIFI Connecting..");

// lcd.setCursor(0,1);

// lcd.print("Please Wait...");

delay(1000);

connect_wifi("AT",1000);

connect_wifi("AT+CWMODE=3",1000);

connect_wifi("AT+CWQAP",1000);

connect_wifi("AT+RST",5000);

check4IP(5000);

if(!No_IP)

    {

    Serial.println("Connecting Wifi....");

    connect_wifi("AT+CWJAP=\"1st
floor\",\"muda1884\"",7000);
//AT+CWJAP="wifi_username","wifi_password"

    }

    else
```

```
{

}

Serial.println("Wifi Connected");

lcd.clear();

lcd.print("WIFI Connected");

delay(2000);

lcd.clear();

lcd.print("Getting IP");

get_ip();

delay(2000);

connect_wifi("AT+CIPMUX=1",100);

connect_wifi("AT+CIPSERVER=1,80",100);

Serial1.end();

lcd.clear();

lcd.print("Waiting For GPS");

lcd.setCursor(0,1);

lcd.print("    Signal    ");

delay(2000);
```

```
gps.begin(9600);

get_gps();

show_coordinate();

gps.end();

Serial1.begin(9600);

delay(2000);

lcd.clear();

lcd.print("GPS is Ready");

delay(1000);

lcd.clear();

lcd.print("System Ready");

Serial.println("System Ready..");
}

void loop()
{
k=0;

Serial.println("Please Refresh Ur Page");

lcd.setCursor(0,0);
```

```
lcd.print("Please Refresh ");

lcd.setCursor(0,1);

lcd.print("Your Web Page.. ");

while(k<1000)

{

 k++;

while(Serial1.available())

{

 if(Serial1.find("0,CONNECT"))

{

   Serial1.end();

gps.begin(9600);

get_gps();

gps.end();

Serial1.begin(9600);

Serial1.flush();

 /* lcd.clear();

   lcd.print("Sending Data to ");
```

```
        lcd.setCursor(0,1);

        lcd.print("    Web Page    ");*/

        Serial.println("Start Printing");

        Send();

        show_coordinate();

        Serial.println("Done Printing");

        delay(5000);

        lcd.clear();

        lcd.print("System Ready");

        delay(1000);

        k=1200;

        break;

        }

    }

    delay(1);

}

}

void gpsEvent()
```

```
{

gpsString="";

while(1)

{

while (gps.available()>0)              //Serial incoming data
from GPS

{

char inChar = (char)gps.read();

gpsString+= inChar;                    //store incoming data
from GPS to temporary string str[]

i++;

if (i < 7)

{

if(gpsString[i-1] != test[i-1])        //check for right string

{

i=0;

gpsString="";

}
```

```
        }
    if(inChar=='\r')
        {
        if(i>65)
            {
            gps_status=1;
            break;
            }
        else
            {
            i=0;
            }
        }
    }
    if(gps_status)
        break;
    }
}
```

```
void get_gps()
{
    gps_status=0;

    int x=0;

    while(gps_status==0)
    {
    gpsEvent();

    int str_lenth=i;

    latitude="";

    logitude="";

    coordinate2dec();

        i=0;x=0;

    str_lenth=0;

    }
}
void show_coordinate()
{
    lcd.clear();
```

```
lcd.print("Latitide:");

lcd.print(latitude);

lcd.setCursor(0,1);

lcd.print("Longitude:");

lcd.print(logitude);

Serial.print("Latitude:");

Serial.println(latitude);

Serial.print("Longitude:");

Serial.println(logitude);
}
void coordinate2dec()
{


//j=0;
String lat_degree="";
for(i=18;i<20;i++)          //extract latitude from string
  lat_degree+=gpsString[i];
```

```
String lat_minut="";

for(i=20;i<28;i++)

  lat_minut+=gpsString[i];


String long_degree="";

for(i=30;i<33;i++)          //extract longitude from string

  long_degree+=gpsString[i];


String long_minut="";

for(i=33;i<41;i++)

  long_minut+=gpsString[i];


float minut= lat_minut.toFloat();

minut=minut/60;

float degree=lat_degree.toFloat();

latitude=degree+minut;


minut= long_minut.toFloat();
```

```cpp
    minut=minut/60;

    degree=long_degree.toFloat();

    logitude=degree+minut;
}
void Send()
{


    webpage = "<h1>Welcome to Saddam Khan's
Page</h1><body bgcolor=f0f0f0>";

    webpage+=name;

    webpage+=dob;

    webpage+=number;

    webpage+=cordinat;

    webpage+="<p>Latitude:";

    webpage+=latitude;

    webpage+="</p>";

    webpage+="<p>Longitude:";

    webpage+=logitude;
```

```
webpage+="</p>";

webpage+=                                    "<a
href=\"http://maps.google.com/maps?&z=15&mrt=yp&t=k
&q=";

webpage+=latitude;

webpage+='+';                    //28.612953,  77.231545
//28.612953,77.2293563

webpage+=logitude;

webpage+="\">Click  Here  for  google  map</a>";

sendwebdata();

 webpage="";
while(1)

  {

  Serial.println("AT+CIPCLOSE=0");

  Serial1.println("AT+CIPCLOSE=0");

  while(Serial1.available())

  {

  //Serial.print(Serial1.read());

  if(Serial1.find("0,CLOSE"))
```

```
        {

          return;

          }

      }

  delay(500);

  i++;

  if(i>5)

      {

        i=0;

      }

  if(i==0)

  break;

      }

}

void sendwebdata()

{

    i=0;

    while(1)
```

```cpp
{
    unsigned int l=webpage.length();

    Serial1.print("AT+CIPSEND=0,");

    Serial1.println(l+2);

    Serial.println(l+2);

    Serial.println(webpage);

Serial1.println(webpage);

    while(Serial1.available())

    {

        if(Serial1.find("OK"))

        {

            return;

        }

    }

        i++;

    if(i>5)

        i=0;

        if(i==0)
```

```
    break;

  delay(200);

    }

  }
```

2.Arduino Smart Watch for Android

DIY smart watch

Designed by Wonho, godstale
http://www.hardcopyworld.com

Keen Watches are mainstream now days and turned out to be significant in the realm of IoT. Keen Watches look cool as well as they are exceptionally helpful as well. In any case, their costs are extremely high and anybody can't bear. So here we are sharing an extremely less expensive arrangement that is Arduino Based Smart Watch. This person TORTUGA made this Smart Watch as an open source venture, and named it Retro Watch.

This Retro Watch can be matched up with your Smart telephone and can demonstrate a wide range of warnings from telephone, as for new messages and messages. It can demonstrate Phone's System data like Battery Status, Wi-Fi status and so forth. It has RSS Feed highlight, and you can utilize it to screen RSS channels from any site like for setting whether conjecture alert. It has many Clock styles to show time and has 65 symbols for presentation warnings. All data is refreshed in like clockwork. This Watch has numerous different highlights.

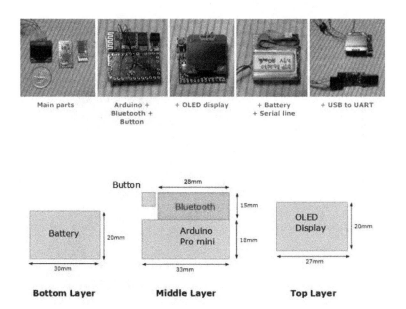

Main parts   Arduino +   + OLED display   + Battery   + USB to UART
Bluetooth +   + Serial line
Button

Button   28mm

Bluetooth   15mm

Battery   Arduino   OLED Display   20mm
20mm   Pro mini   18mm

30mm   33mm   27mm

Bottom Layer   **Middle Layer**   **Top Layer**

This Smart Watch is for the most part utilizing Arduino Pro Mini, 128x64 OLED realistic presentation, HC-06 Bluetooth

Module, LiPo (Lithium-Polymer) battery and a FTDI Module. These segments are stacked one over another, to make it minimal, having encasing dark tape in the middle of each 'layer'. OLED and Bluetooth module are associated with Arduino Pro Mini. Arduino Pro Mini is utilized in view of its little size. A Button is associated with Arduino to fill in as Momentary Reset Switch for Smart Watch.

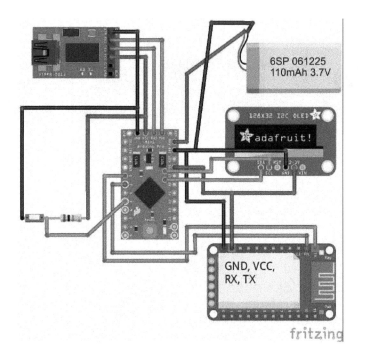

Source Code for Arduino and Android application for Smart telephone have been given in the instructional exercise. This DIY Tutorial discloses each progression to fabricate this Smart telephone. FTDI Friend is utilized to Burn the code into Arduino Pro Mini from PC. You have to introduce OLED Adafruit Graphic library before consuming the code. So now you simply need to match your advanced cell's Bluetooth to the Bluetooth module, associated with Arduino and you are prepared to go.

This Clock is additionally improved here by Bryan Smith as Helios Watch (demonstrated as follows) with bigger screen vibration inside battery charging and so forth.

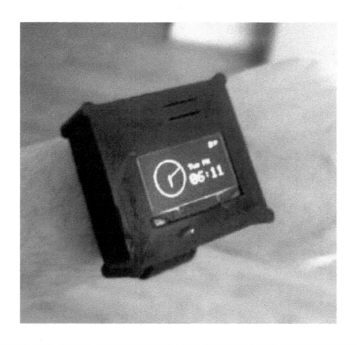

3.How to Send Data from Arduino to Webpage using WiFi

Remote correspondence between Electronic gadgets and modules is significant, to make them 'Fit' in the World of Internet of Things. HTTP convention and HTML language have made it conceivable to move the Data anyplace on the planet, over the web. We have officially secured a few undertakings which use Wi-Fi with Arduino, view them to Getting started :

1. Sending Email utilizing Arduino and ESP8266 WiFi Module

2. WiFi Controlled Robot utilizing Arduino

3. Controlling RGB LED utilizing Arduino and Wi-Fi

Presently in this instructional exercise, we are building a program to Send Data to Web utilizing Arduino as well as Wi-Fi module. For this we first need an IP address of either Global or Local server, here for the straightforwardness and exhibit reason, we are utilizing Local Server.

Components Required:

1. ESP8266 Wi-Fi Module
2. Arduino UNO
3. USB Cable
4. Laptop
5. Connecting wires
6. Power supply

Wi-Fi Module ESP8266:

Circuit Connections:

Circuit Diagram for "Post Data since Arduino to Web" is given beneath. We mostly need an Arduino as well as ESP8266 Wi-Fi module. ESP8266's Vcc and GND pins are straightforwardly associated with 3.3V and GND of Arduino and CH_PD is likewise associated with 3.3V. Tx as well as Rx pins of ESP8266 are straightforwardly associated with stick 2 and 3 of Arduino. Programming Serial Library is utilized to permit sequential correspondence on stick 2 and 3 of Arduino. We have officially secured the Interfacing of ESP8266 Wi-Fi module to Arduino in detail.

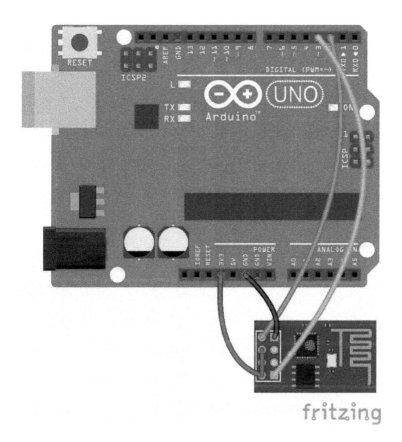

By utilizing Software Serial Library here, we have permitted sequential correspondence on stick 2 and 3, and made them Rx and Tx individually. As a matter of course Pin 0 and 1 of Arduino are utilized for sequential correspondence yet by utilizing SoftwareSerial library, we can permit sequential correspondence on other advanced pins of the Arduino.

Note: To watch the reaction of ESP8266 on sequential screen, kindly open Serial Monitor of Arduino IDE.

Working Explanation:

Above all else we have to interface our Wi-Fi module to Wi-Fi switch for system network. At that point we will Configure the neighborhood server, Send the information to Web lastly Close the association. This procedure and directions have been clarified in beneath steps:

1. First we have to test the Wi-Fi module by sending AT order, it will return a reaction containing OK.

2. After this, we have to choose mode utilizing order AT+CWMODE=mode_id , we have utilized Mode id =3. Mode ids:

1 = Station mode (customer)

2 = AP mode (have)

3 = AP + Station mode (Yes, ESP8266 have a double mode!)

3. Presently we have to detach our Wi-Fi module from the recently associated Wi-Fi organize, by utilizing the direction AT+CWQAP, as ESP8266 is default auto associated with any already accessible Wi-Fi arrange

4. From that point forward, client can Reset the module with AT+RST direction. This progression is discretionary.

5. Presently we have to interface ESP8266 to Wi-Fi switch utilizing given order

AT+CWJAP="wifi_username","wifi_password"

6. Presently get IP Address by utilizing given order:

AT+CIFSR

It will restore an IP Address.

7. Presently empower the multiplex mode by utilizing AT+CIPMUX=1 (1 for various association and 0 for single association)

8. By and by mastermind ESP8266 as server by using AT+CIPSERVER=1,port_no (port may be 80). By and by your Wi-Fi is readied. Here '1' is utilized to make the server and '0' to erase the server.

9. Presently by utilizing given order client can send information to nearby made server:

AT+CIPSEND =id, length of information

Id = ID no. of transmit association

Length = Max length of information is 2 kb

10. In the wake of sending ID and Length to the server, we have to send information like : Serial.println("your_mail@gmail.com");

11. In the wake of sending information we need close the association by given direction:

AT+CIPCLOSE=0

Presently information has been transmitted to nearby server.

12. Presently type IP Address at Address Bar at internet browser as well as hit enter. Presently client can see transmitted information on site page.

Steps for Programming:

1. Incorporate SoftwareSerial Library for permit sequential correspondence on PIN 2 and 3 and proclaim a few factors and strings.

```
#include<SoftwareSerial.h>

SoftwareSerial client(2,3); //RX, TX

String webpage="";

int i=0,k=0;

String readString;
```

```
int x=0;

boolean No_IP=false;

String IP="";

char temp1='0';
```

2. After this, we need to characterize a few capacities for playing out our ideal errands.

In Setup() work, we initialise inbuilt sequential UART correspondence for ESP8266 as client.begin(9600); at the baud pace of 9600.

```
void setup()

{

    Serial.begin(9600);

    client.begin(9600);

    wifi_init();
```

```
Serial.println("System Ready..");

}
```

3. In wifi_init() work, we introduce the wifi module by sending a few directions like reset, set mode, interface with switch, arrange association and so on. These directions have likewise been clarified above in portrayal part.

```
void wifi_init()

{

    connect_wifi("AT",100);

    connect_wifi("AT+CWMODE=3",100);

    connect_wifi("AT+CWQAP",100);

    connect_wifi("AT+RST",5000);

    ...... ......

    ..... .....
```

4. In connect_wifi() work, we send directions information to ESP8266 and afterward read reaction from ESP8266 Wi-Fi module.

```
void connect_wifi(String cmd, int t)

{

int temp=0,i=0;

while(1)

{

Serial.println(cmd);

...... .....

...... .....
```

5. sendwebdata( ) capacity is utilized for sending information to Local Server or Webpage.

```
void sendwebdata(String webPage)

{

    int ii=0;


    while(1)

    {

    unsigned int l=webPage.length();

    Serial.print("AT+CIPSEND=0,");

    client.print("AT+CIPSEND=0,");

    ...... .....

    ..... .....
```

6. void send() work is utilized for sending information strings to sendwebdata() work. That will be additionally sent to page.

```
void Send()

{

    webpage = "<h1>Welcome  </h1><body bgcolor=f0 f0 f0
>";

    sendwebdata(webpage);

    webpage=name;

    webpage+=dat;

    ...... .....

    ..... .....
```

7. get_ip() work is utilized for getting IP address of Local made server.

8. In void circle() work, we send guidance to client for invigorating the page and check whether the server is associated of not. At the point when client revive or demand the website page, information naturally transmitted to a similar IP address.

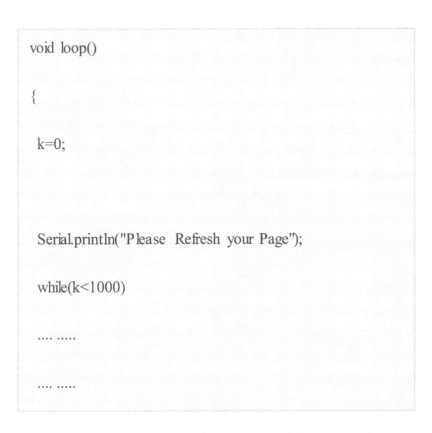

```
void loop()

{

k=0;

Serial.println("Please Refresh your Page");

while(k<1000)

.... .....

.... .....
```

We can show any information from Arduino to Webpage utilizing this procedure, similar to Room Temperature and Humidity, Clock time, GPS organizes, Heart beat Rate and so forth.

Code

#include<SoftwareSerial.h>

```
SoftwareSerial client(2,3);  //RX, TX

String webpage="";

int i=0,k=0;

String readString;

int x=0;

boolean No_IP=false;

String IP="";

char temp1='0';

String name="<p>hello_world</p>";   //22

String dat="<p>Data Received Successfully.....</p>";
//21


void check4IP(int t1)

{

  int t2=millis();

  while(t2+t1>millis())

  {

    while(client.available()>0)
```

```
        {

        if(client.find("WIFI  GOT IP"))

          {

          No_IP=true;

          }

        }

      }

    }

void get_ip()

{

  IP="";

  char ch=0;

  while(1)

  {

    client.println("AT+CIFSR");

    while(client.available()>0)

    {

      if(client.find("STAIP,"))
```

```
{
    delay(1000);

    Serial.print("IP   Address:");

    while(client.available()>0)
    {
        ch=client.read();

        if(ch=='+')

        break;

        IP+=ch;
    }
}

if(ch=='+')

break;
}

if(ch=='+')

break;

delay(1000);
}
```

```
Serial.print(IP);

Serial.print("Port:");

Serial.println(80);

}

void connect_wifi(String cmd, int t)

{

  int temp=0,i=0;

  while(1)

  {

    Serial.println(cmd);

    client.println(cmd);

    while(client.available())

    {

      if(client.find("OK"))

      i=8;

    }

    delay(t);

    if(i>5)
```

```
        break;

       i++;

      }

    if(i==8)

    Serial.println("OK");

    else

    Serial.println("Error");

   }

  void wifi_init()

  {

      connect_wifi("AT",100);

      connect_wifi("AT+CWMODE=3",100);

      connect_wifi("AT+CWQAP",100);

      connect_wifi("AT+RST",5000);

      check4IP(5000);

      if(!No_IP)

      {

        Serial.println("Connecting Wifi....");
```

```
connect_wifi("AT+CWJAP=\"1st
floor\",\"muda1884\"",7000);        //provide your WiFi
username and password here

// connect_wifi("AT+CWJAP=\"vpn
address\",\"wireless network\"",7000);

}

else

{

}

Serial.println("Wifi Connected");

get_ip();

connect_wifi("AT+CIPMUX=1",100);

connect_wifi("AT+CIPSERVER=1,80",100);

}

void sendwebdata(String webPage)

{

int ii=0;

while(1)
```

```
{
    unsigned  int l=webPage.length();
    Serial.print("AT+CIPSEND=0,");
    client.print("AT+CIPSEND=0,");
    Serial.println(l+2);
    client.println(l+2);
    delay(100);
    Serial.println(webPage);
    client.println(webPage);
    while(client.available())
    {
      //Serial.print(Serial.read());
      if(client.find("OK"))
      {
        ii=11;
        break;
      }
    }
```

```
if(ii==11)

break;

delay(100);

    }

}

void setup()

{

  Serial.begin(9600);

  client.begin(9600);

  wifi_init();

  Serial.println("System Ready..");

}

void loop()

{

  k=0;

  Serial.println("Please Refresh your Page");

  while(k<1000)

  {
```

```
k++;

while(client.available())

{

if(client.find("0,CONNECT"))

{

  Serial.println("Start Printing");

  Send();

  Serial.println("Done Printing");

  delay(1000);

}

}

delay(1);

}

}

void Send()

{

    webpage = "<h1>Welcome </h1><body
bgcolor=f0f0f0>";
```

```
sendwebdata(webpage);

webpage=name;

webpage+=dat;

sendwebdata(webpage);

delay(1000);

webpage = "<a href="http://your_mail.com/";

webpage+="\">Click Here for More projects</a>";

sendwebdata(webpage);

client.println("AT+CIPCLOSE=0");

}
```

4.Controlling RGB LED using Arduino and Wi-Fi

In last instructional exercise, we clarified controlling a Robot utilizing Wi-Fi as well as Arduino, as well as our next IOT Project-RGB LED Flasher utilizing Wi-Fi. Here we have utilized Arduino and ESP8266 Wi-Fi Module to control the shades of RGB LED, through an Android Phone, over the Wi-Fi.

In this RGB Flasher LED, we have utilized an Android Mobile App named "Blynk". Blynk is a truly good application with Arduino, to make IoT based task. This App can be downloaded from the Google Play Store, and can be effectively designed.

Step for configuring Blynk App:

1. First download it from Google Play Store and introduce it in Android cell phone.

2. After this, it is required to make a record. You may utilize your current Gmail account.

3. Presently select Arduino Board and give a name for your task.

4. Note the Auth Token Code instead essentially mail it to your Email Account as well as afterward reorder in Arduino sketch (Program Code).

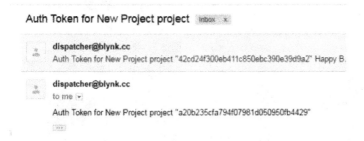

Auth Token for New Project project Inbox x

dispatcher@blynk.cc
Auth Token for New Project project "42cd24f300eb411c850ebc390e39d9a2" Happy B.

dispatcher@blynk.cc
to me

Auth Token for New Project project "a20b235cfa794f07981d050950fb4429"

5. Enter this Auth Token Code in Arduino sketch.

// You should get Auth Token in the Blynk App.

// Go to the Project Settings (nut icon).

char auth[] = "a20b235cfa794f07981d050950fb4429";

6. At that point click on make catch in Blynk application.

7. Presently Select the Large Slider and two catches, arrange them and hit the back catch.

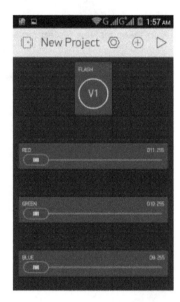

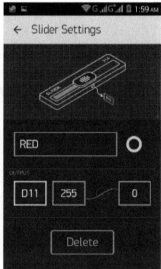

 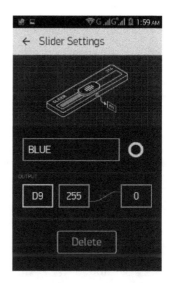

8. After it press Play catch at the correct top of screen.

Required Components:

1. Arduino UNO
2. ESP8266 Wi-Fi Module
3. USB Cable
4. Connecting wires
5. RGB LED
6. Android Mobile phone
7. Blynk App

Circuit and Working Explanation:

RGB LED Flasher diagram is given underneath. We essentially need an Arduino, ESP8266 Wi-Fi module as well as RGB LED. ESP8266's Vcc and GND pins are straightforwardly associated with 3.3V and GND of Arduino and CH_PD is additionally associated with 3.3V. Tx as well as Rx pins of ESP8266 are straightforwardly associated with stick 2 and 3 of Arduino. Programming Serial Library is utilized to permit sequential correspondence on stick 2 and 3 of Arduino. We have effectively secured the Interfacing of ESP8266 Wi-Fi module to Arduino in detail.

Here we have utilized a Common Anode RGB LED. This RGB LED sticks in particular R, G, B and anode are associated at 11, 10, 9 and +5 volt Vcc. Normal Anode stick has a 1K resistor with +5 volt for securing the LED to be harmed.

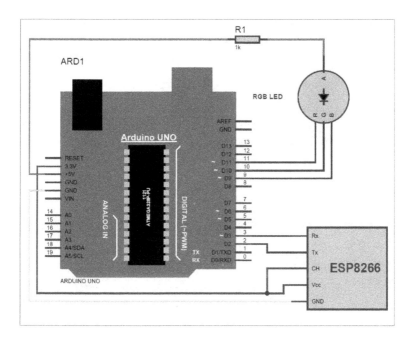

Working of the RGB LED is basic, we have made three Sliders, utilizing Blynk application, for controlling the force of three shades of RGB LED that is RED, GREEN and BLUE. What's more, one catch for Flashing the RGB LED in various example, as per Program code.

Programming Explanation:

First we have to download and introduce Blynk Library for Arduino.

We have incorporated all the required libraries to run this code in Arduino IDE, as well as after that entered Auth Token, from the Blynk application, in the auth string. Here we are interfacing Wi-Fi sequential stick with Software Serial of Arduino. Chosen stick 2 as RX and 3 as TX.

```
#define BLYNK_PRINT Serial    // Comment this out to disable prints as well as save space

#include <ESP8266_SoftSer.h>



#include <BlynkSimpleShieldEsp8266_SoftSer.h>



// Set ESP8266 Serial object

#include <SoftwareSerial.h>

SoftwareSerial EspSerial(2, 3); // RX, TX
```

```
ESP8266 wifi(EspSerial);
```

```
// You should get Auth Token in the Blynk App.

// Go to the Project Settings (nut icon).

char auth[] = "a20b235cfa794f07981d050950fb4429";
```

After it we have characterized yield pins for RGB LED

```
#define red 11


#define green 10

#define blue 9
```

After this, in arrangement work we introduce all the required gadgets, start sequential correspondence, giving Wi-Fi username and secret word.

```
void setup()

{

// Set console baud rate

Serial.begin(9600);

delay(10);


// Set ESP8266 baud rate

// 9600 is recommended for Software Serial

EspSerial.begin(9600);

delay(10);


Blynk.begin(auth, wifi, "username", "password");  // wifi u
sername and password

}
```

At that point we have checked condition for Button (Virtual Pin 1). Here we have chosen virtual stick 1 (V1) for taking contribution from Blynk App to streak the RGB LED.

We should take note of that, we have appended two codes in our Code area beneath, initial one is only for controlling the power of three hues in RGB LED without glimmering it and second one is for blazing the LED just as controlling the three shades of RGB LED. We just need to characterize RGB Led sticks in second program, for example Glimmering LED program, since Flashing of LED is constrained by Arduino. Then again in first program, Colors of LED is constrained by Blynk application in Android telephone, so we don't have to characterize RGB LED pins.

We can say that in case that we just need to change the shading by Sliders and would prefer not to utilize Button for flasher then we don't have to characterize of RGB pins.

The given capacity is for glimmering the RGB LED when catch is squeezed from the Blynk App.

BLYNK_WRITE(V1)

```
{

  int x = param[0].asInt();


  while(x==1)

  {

  x = param.asInt();

  int i=0,j=0,k=0;

  analogWrite(red,  255);


  analogWrite(green,  255);

  ... .....


  .... .....
```

Finally we have to run blynk work in circle, to run the framework.

```
void loop()

{

  Blynk.run();

}
```

Note: Two Codes have been given beneath. One is for simply changing the shades of RGB LED without flasher as well as second one is for changing the hues with Flasher.

Code

Code 1: Change the colors of RGB LED without Flasher

#define BLYNK_PRINT Serial   // Comment this out to disable prints and save space

#include <ESP8266_SoftSer.h>

#include <BlynkSimpleShieldEsp8266_SoftSer.h>

// Set ESP8266 Serial object

#include <SoftwareSerial.h>

SoftwareSerial EspSerial(2, 3); // RX, TX

ESP8266 wifi(EspSerial);

```
// You should get Auth Token in the Blynk App.
// Go to the Project Settings (nut icon).
char auth[] = "a20b235cfa794f07981d050950fb4429";

void setup()
{
  // Set console baud rate
  Serial.begin(9600);
  delay(10);
  // Set ESP8266 baud rate
  // 9600 is recommended for Software Serial
  EspSerial.begin(9600);
  delay(10);
Blynk.begin(auth, wifi, "1st floor", "muda1884");
}
void loop()
{
  Blynk.run();
}
```

Code 2: Change the colors of RGB LED with Flasher

```
#define BLYNK_PRINT Serial    // Comment this out to
disable prints and save space
```

```
#include <ESP8266_SoftSer.h>
#include <BlynkSimpleShieldEsp8266_SoftSer.h>

// Set ESP8266 Serial object
#include <SoftwareSerial.h>
SoftwareSerial EspSerial(2, 3); // RX, TX

ESP8266 wifi(EspSerial);

// You should get Auth Token in the Blynk App.
// Go to the Project Settings (nut icon).
char auth[] = "a20b235cfa794f07981d050950fb4429";

#define red 11
#define green 10
#define blue 9

void setup()
{
  // Set console baud rate
  Serial.begin(9600);
  delay(10);
  // Set ESP8266 baud rate
  // 9600 is recommended for Software Serial
  EspSerial.begin(9600);
  delay(10);
```

```
Blynk.begin(auth, wifi, "username", "password");   // wifi
username and password
}
BLYNK_WRITE(V1)
{
 int x = param[0].asInt();

   while(x==1)
   {
   x = param.asInt();
   int i=0,j=0,k=0;
   analogWrite(red, 255);
   analogWrite(green, 255);
   analogWrite(blue, 255);

     for(int j=0;j<20;j++)
     {
     analogWrite(red, 0);
     analogWrite(green, 255);
     analogWrite(blue, 255);
     delay(100);
     analogWrite(red, 255);
     analogWrite(green, 0);
     analogWrite(blue, 255);
```

```
delay(100);
analogWrite(red, 255);
analogWrite(green, 255);
analogWrite(blue, 0);
delay(100);
 x = param.asInt();
 if(x==0)
 break;
}


analogWrite(red, 255);
analogWrite(green, 255);
analogWrite(blue, 255);

for(int z=0;z<10;z++)
{
for(i=0;i<=180;i++)
{
    analogWrite(red, 180-i);
    delay(2);
}
analogWrite(red, 255);
for(j=0;j<255;j++)
{
```

```
        analogWrite(green,  255-j);
        delay(2);
}
analogWrite(green,  255);
for(k=0;k<255;k++)
{
        analogWrite(blue,  255-k);
        delay(2);
}
analogWrite(blue,  255);
 x = param.asInt();
 if(x==0)
 break;


}


analogWrite(red,  255);
analogWrite(green,  255);
analogWrite(blue,  255);
    for(int  z=0;z<5;z++)
{
for(j=0;j<255;j++)
{
        analogWrite(green,  255-j);
```

```
            delay(20);
    }
    for(k=0;k<255;k++)
    {
        analogWrite(blue,  255-k);
        delay(20);
    }


      for(i=0;i<=180;i++)
    {
        analogWrite(red,  180-i);
        delay(20);
    }
    analogWrite(red,180);
    x = param.asInt();
    if(x==0)
    break;
    }
    if(x==0)
    break;
    }
    analogWrite(red,  255);
    analogWrite(green,  255);
```

```
    analogWrite(blue,  255);

}

void loop()

{

 Blynk.run();

}
```

5.Sending Email using Arduino and ESP8266 WiFi Module

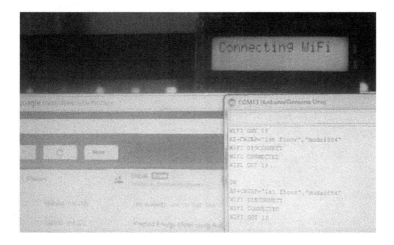

We are moving towards the World of IoT. This innovation assumes a significant job in the Electronics and Embedded framework. Sending an Email from any Microcontroller or Embedded framework is fundamental thing, which is required in IoT. So in this article, we will realize "How to send an Email utilizing Wi-Fi and Arduino".

For sending Email through Wi-Fi module and Arduino, as a matter of first importance we need an Email account. So client can make email account at smtp2go.com. After information exchange, recall your new email address and secret phrase.

We can comprehend the entire procedure in underneath Steps:

Stage 1: First mastermind all the required Components.

1. Arduino UNO
2. ESP8266 Wi-Fi module
3. USB Cable
4. Laptop
5. 16x2 LCD (optional)
6. 10K POT (optional)
7. Power supply
8. Connecting wires

Wi-Fi Module ESP8266:

Stage 2: In this progression we will associate ESP8266 Wi-Fi module with Arduino and give it power supply from 3.3v stick of Arduino.

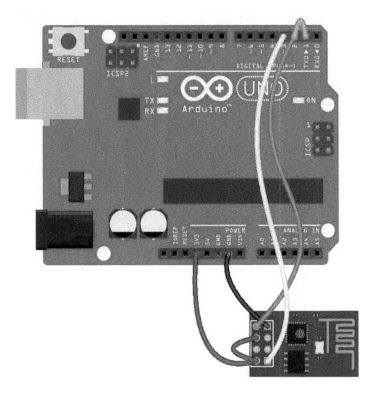

Stage 3: In this progression, we have to pursue Email address and Password (smtp2go.com). smtp2go.com gives the email administrations, to send the messages utilizing active email server.

Stage 4: We will require Username and Password in base64 encoded position with utf-8 character set. For changing over the Email and Password in base64 encoded organization use beneath given connection. Keep the encoded username as well as secret key convenient, we need it in our program to login at smtp2go.com.

https://www.base64encode.org/

Stage 5: Now begin composing code for sending Email. 'Programming Explanation' and Code is given toward the end.

Circuit Explanation:

Circuit is exceptionally basic, for this task we just need Arduino as well as ESP8266 Wi-Fi module. A 16x2 LCD is likewise associated for showing the status messages. This LCD is discretionary. ESP8266's Vcc and GND pins are straightforwardly associated with 3.3V and GND of Arduino and CH_PD is additionally associated with 3.3V.

Tx as well as Rx pins of ESP8266 are straightforwardly associated with stick 2 and 3 of Arduino. What's more, Pin 2 of Arduino is likewise shorted with Tx stick (Pin 1) of Arduino. This stick is shorted for showing reaction of ESP8266 legitimately on Serial screen of Arduino. Programming Serial Library is utilized to permit sequential correspondence on stick 2 and 3 of Arduino.

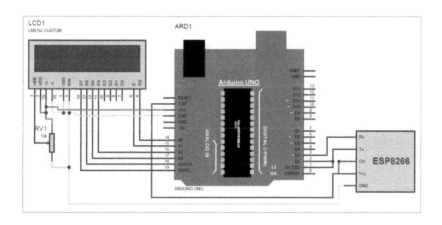

Note: For viewing the reaction of ESP8266 on Serial Monitor, don't initialise the Serial.begin(9600) work.

Programming Explanation:

1. In programming part first we incorporate libraries and characterize pins for LCD and programming sequential correspondence. As a matter of course Pin 0 and 1 of Arduino are utilized for sequential correspondence yet by utilizing SoftwareSerial library, we can permit sequential correspondence on other advanced pins of the Arduino.

2. void connect_wifi(String cmd, int t) Function is characterized to Connect the Wi-Fi module to the Internet.

```
void connect_wifi(String cmd, int t)

{



int temp=0,i=0;

while(1)

{

Serial1.println(cmd);
```

```
while(Serial1.available())

{



  if(Serial1.find("OK"))


    ... .... ....

    ... ......
```

3. After it associate module to SMTP server by utilizing given directions:

```
lcd.print("Configuring Email..");

 Serial1.println("AT+CIPSTART=4,\"TCP\",\"mail.smtp2
go.com\",2525");

 delay(2000);

Serial1.println("AT+CIPSEND=4,20");

 delay(2000);
```

```
Seriall.println("EHLO  192.168.1.123");

delay(2000);

Seriall.println("AT+CIPSEND=4,12");
```

Note: Many email servers won't acknowledge email from a non-business, dhcp-issued ip address.

4. Presently we will attempt to Login at smtp2go.co, utilizing the base64 encoded User name and secret phrase, which we have inferred in Step 4 above.

```
lcd.print("Try To Login.....");



Seriall.println("AUTH  LOGIN");

delay(2000);

Seriall.println("AT+CIPSEND=4,30");

delay(2000);
```

```
Serial1.println("c2FkZGFtNDIwMUBnbWFpbC5jb20=");
//base64 encoded username

delay(2000);



Serial1.println("AT+CIPSEND=4,18");

delay(2000);

Serial1.println("Y21yY3VpdDQyMDE=");          //base
64 encoded password
```

5. After this, enter your principle message that client need to send. Also, send this email by completion line (sending) '.'

```
Serial1.println("Testing Success");

delay(2000);

Serial1.println("AT+CIPSEND=4,3");

delay(2000);
```

```
Serial1.println('.');

delay(10000);

Serial1.println("AT+CIPSEND=4,6");

delay(2000);

Serial1.println("QUIT");

... .....

.......
```

Different capacities and Code are clear as crystal and straightforward.

Code

```
#include<LiquidCrystal.h>
LiquidCrystal lcd(14,15,16,17,18,19);
#include <SoftwareSerial.h>
SoftwareSerial Serial1(2, 3); // RX, TX
boolean No_IP=false;
String IP="";
```

```
void check4IP(int t1)
{
  int t2=millis();
  Serial1.flush();
  while(t2+t1>millis())
  {
    while(Serial1.available()>0)
    {
      if(Serial1.find("WIFI  GOT IP"))
      {
        No_IP=true;
      }
    }
  }
}
void get_ip()
{
  IP="";
  char ch=0;
  while(1)
  {
    Serial1.println("AT+CIFSR");
    while(Serial1.available()>0)
    {
```

```
    if(Serial1.find("STAIP,"))
    {
      delay(1000);
      Serial.print("IP  Address:");
      while(Serial1.available()>0)
      {
       ch=Serial1.read();
       if(ch=='+')
       break;
       IP+=ch;
      }
     }
    if(ch=='+')
    break;
    }
  if(ch=='+')
  break;
  delay(1000);
  }
 Serial.print(IP);
 Serial.print("Port:");
 Serial.println(80);
}
```

```
void connect_wifi(String cmd, int t)
{
  int temp=0,i=0;
  while(1)
  {
    Serial1.println(cmd);
    while(Serial1.available())
    {
      if(Serial1.find("OK"))
      i=8;
    }
    delay(t);
    if(i>5)
    break;
    i++;
  }
  if(i==8)
  Serial.println("OK");
  else
  Serial.println("Error");
}
void setup()
{
  Serial1.begin(9600);
```

```
// Serial.begin(9600);
lcd.begin(16,2);
lcd.print("Sending Email by");
lcd.setCursor(0,1);
lcd.print(" Arduino & WIFI ");
delay(2000);
lcd.clear();
lcd.print(" Hello_world");
delay(2000);
lcd.clear();
lcd.print("Finding ESP8266");
connect_wifi("AT",100);
connect_wifi("ATE1",100);
lcd.clear();
lcd.print("Connected");
delay(1000);
connect_wifi("AT+CWMODE=3",100);
connect_wifi("AT+CWQAP",100);
connect_wifi("AT+RST",5000);
lcd.clear();
lcd.print("Connecting WiFi");
check4IP(5000);
if(!No_IP)
{
```

```
Serial.println("Connecting Wifi....");
connect_wifi("AT+CWJAP=\"1st
floor\",\"muda1884\"",7000);    //provide your WiFi
username and password here
}
else
{

}
lcd.clear();
lcd.print("WIFI Connected...");
Serial.println("Wifi Connected");
delay(1000);
lcd.clear();
lcd.print("Getting IP Add.");
Serial.println("Getting IP Address....");
get_ip();
delay(1000);
lcd.clear();
lcd.print("IP:");
lcd.print(IP);
lcd.setCursor(0,1);
lcd.print("PORT: 80");
connect_wifi("AT+CIPMUX=1",100);
connect_wifi("AT+CIPSERVER=1,80",100);
```

```
delay(2000);
lcd.clear();
lcd.print("Configuring Email..");
Seriall.println("AT+CIPSTART=4,\"TCP\",\"mail.smtp2
go.com\",2525");
delay(2000);
Seriall.println("AT+CIPSEND=4,20");
delay(2000);
Seriall.println("EHLO 192.168.1.123");
delay(2000);
Seriall.println("AT+CIPSEND=4,12");
delay(2000);
lcd.clear();
lcd.print("Try To Login.....");
Seriall.println("AUTH LOGIN");
delay(2000);
Seriall.println("AT+CIPSEND=4,30");
delay(2000);
Seriall.println("c2FkZGFtNDIwMUBnbWFpbC5jb20=");
//base64 encoded username
delay(2000);
Seriall.println("AT+CIPSEND=4,18");
delay(2000);
Seriall.println("Y21yY3VpdDQyMDE=");              //b
```

```
ase64 encoded password
lcd.clear();
lcd.print("Login Success");
delay(2000);
Serial1.println("AT+CIPSEND=4,34");
delay(2000);
Serial1.println("MAIL
FROM:<saddam4201@ gmail.com>");  // use your email
address
delay(2000);
Serial1.println("AT+CIPSEND=4,32");
delay(2000);
lcd.clear();
lcd.print("Seniding Email 2");
lcd.setCursor(0,1);
lcd.print("Saddam4201@ gmail");
Serial1.println("RCPT To:<saddam4201@ gmail.com>");
delay(2000);
Serial1.println("AT+CIPSEND=4,6");
delay(2000);
Serial1.println("DATA");
delay(2000);
Serial1.println("AT+CIPSEND=4,24");
delay(2000);
```

```
Serial1.println("Testing Success");
delay(2000);
Serial1.println("AT+CIPSEND=4,3");
delay(2000);
Serial1.println('.');
delay(10000);
Serial1.println("AT+CIPSEND=4,6");
delay(2000);
Serial1.println("QUIT");
delay(2000);
lcd.clear();
lcd.print("Email Sent...");
}

void loop()
{


}
```

6.WiFi Controlled Robot using Arduino

There are numerous sorts of Robots, from the basic ones like a Toy vehicle to the propelled ones like mechanical Robots. We have effectively secured numerous kinds of Robots utilizing various advances, examine them:

1. Line Follower Robot utilizing 8051 Microcontroller

2. Line Follower Robot utilizing Arduino

3. DTMF Controlled Robot utilizing Arduino

4. Phone Controlled Robot utilizing 8051 Microcontroller

5. PC Controlled Robot utilizing Arduino

6. RF Controlled Robot

7. Edge Avoiding Robot Using 8051

8. Accelerometer Based Hand Gesture Controlled Robot utilizing Arduino

9. Bluetooth Controlled Toy Car utilizing Arduino

Furthermore, presently we are including one more Robot in our 'Mechanical technology Projects' area, this time we are going to make a Wi-Fi controlled Robot utilizing Arduino and Blynk App. This Arduino based Robot can be controlled remotely utilizing any Wi-Fi empowered Android advanced mobile phone.

For show of Wi-Fi Controlled Robot, we have utilized an Android Mobile App named "Blynk". Blynk is a truly perfect application with Arduino, to make IoT based undertaking. This App can be installed from the Google Play Store, as well as can be effectively arranged.

Steps for configuring Blynk App:

1. First download it from Google Play Store and introduce it in Android cell phone.

2. After this, it is required to make a record. You may utilize your current Gmail account.

3. Presently select Arduino Board and give a name for your undertaking.

4. Note the Auth Token Code or basically mail to your Email Account as well as afterward reorder in Arduino sketch (Program Code).

5. Enter this Auth Token Code in Arduino sketch.

```
// You should get Auth Token in the Blynk App.

// Go to the Project Settings (nut icon).

char auth[] = "caa17a11c0124d4083d0eaa995f45917";
```

6. At that point click on make catch in Blynk application.

7. Presently Select the Joystick Widget, Click on Joystick, Configure the Joystick and hit the back catch.

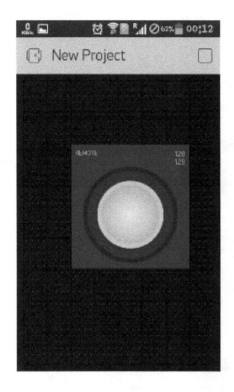

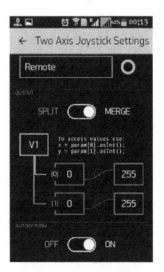

8. After it press Play catch at the correct top of screen.

Required Components:

1. Arduino UNO
2. ESP8266 Wi-Fi Module
3. USB Cable
4. Connecting wires
5. L293D
6. DC Motors
7. Batteries
8. 10K POT (optional)
9. Robot chassis plus wheel
10. Roller caster
11. Android Mobile phone
12. Blynk App

Circuit Explanation:

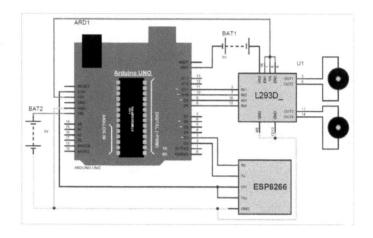

Circuit Diagram of Wi-Fi controlled robot is given underneath. We basically need an Arduino and ESP8266 Wi-Fi module. ESP8266's Vcc and GND pins are straightforwardly associated with 3.3V and GND of Arduino and CH_PD is likewise associated with 3.3V. Tx and Rx pins of ESP8266 are legitimately associated with stick 2 and 3 of Arduino. Programming Serial Library is utilized to permit sequential correspondence on stick 2 and 3 of Arduino. We have officially secured the Interfacing of ESP8266 Wi-Fi module to Arduino in detail.

A L293D Motor Driver IC is utilized for driving DC engines. Info pins of engine driver IC is legitimately associated with stick 8, 9, 10 and 11 of Arduino. Furthermore, DC engines are associated at its yield pins. Here we have utilized 9 Volt battery for driving the Circuit and DC engines.

Working Explanation:

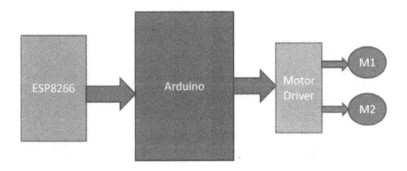

Working of the Wi-Fi controlled Robot is simple, we simply need to Drag or Slide the Joystick toward the path, where we need to move the Robot. Like on the off chance that we have to move the Robot Forward way, at that point we have to Drag the Joystick 'hover' in Forward heading. Similarly move the Robot in Left, Right and Backward course by Dragging the joystick separate way. Presently when we discharge the Joystick, it will return to focus and Robot stops.

Blynk App sends values from Two Axis Joystick to Arduino, through Wi-Fi medium. Arduino get the qualities, contrast them and predefined qualities and move the Robot as needs be toward that path.

Programming Explanation:

Program is nearly readymade accessible in Arduino IDE. We simply need to install Blynk Library for Arduino. What's more, in the wake of making a few adjustments, client can make possess Wi-Fi controlled robot.

First we have incorporated all the required libraries to run this code in Arduino IDE, and afterward entered Auth Token, from the Blynk application, in the auth string. Here we are interfacing Wi-Fi sequential stick with Software Serial of Arduino. Chosen stick 2 as RX and 3 as TX.

```
#define BLYNK_PRINT Serial    // Comment this out to dis
able prints and save space

#include <ESP8266_SoftSer.h>

#include <BlynkSimpleShieldEsp8266_SoftSer.h>
```

```
// Set ESP8266 Serial objec

#include <SoftwareSerial.h>

SoftwareSerial EspSerial(2, 3); // RX, TX

ESP8266 wifi(EspSerial);

// You should get Auth Token in the Blynk App.

// Go to the Project Settings (nut icon).

char auth[] = "caa17a11c0124d4083d0eaa995f45917";
```

At that point we characterized yield pins(8,9,10,11) for engines and thought of some course capacities to move the Robot specifically bearing: void forward(), void backward(),void right() and void left()

After this, in arrangement work we initialise all the required gadgets, such as provide guidance to engine pins, start sequential correspondence, giving Wi-Fi username and secret phrase.

```
void setup()

{

// Set console baud rate

Serial.begin(9600);

delay(10);

// Set ESP8266 baud rate

// 9600 is recommended for Software Serial

EspSerial.begin(9600);

delay(10);


Blynk.begin(auth, wifi, "username", "password"); // wifi
username and password

pinMode(ml1, OUTPUT);

pinMode(ml2, OUTPUT);
```

```
pinMode(m21, OUTPUT);

pinMode(m22, OUTPUT);

}
```

Presently we have checked a few conditions for controlling the robot. Here we have chosen virtual stick 1 (V1) for taking contribution from Blynk App to control the robot. As we have utilized marge alternative in application so we will get x and y hub esteems at same stick.

```
BLYNK_WRITE(V1)

{

int x = param[0].asInt();

int y = param[1].asInt();

if(y>220)

forward();

else if(y<35)
```

```
backward();

else if(x>220)

right();

else if(x<35)

left();

else

Stop();

}
```

Finally we have to run blynk work in circle, to run the framework.

```
void loop()


{
```

```
  Blynk.run();

}
```

Code

```
#define BLYNK_PRINT Serial   // Comment this out to
disable prints and save space
#include <ESP8266_SoftSer.h>
#include <BlynkSimpleShieldEsp8266_SoftSer.h>
// Set ESP8266 Serial object
#include <SoftwareSerial.h>
SoftwareSerial EspSerial(2, 3); // RX, TX
ESP8266 wifi(EspSerial);
// You should get Auth Token in the Blynk App.
// Go to the Project Settings (nut icon).
char auth[] = "caa17a11c0124d4083d0eaa995f45917";
#define ml1 8
#define ml2 9
#define m21 10
#define m22 11
void forward()
{
  digitalWrite(ml1, HIGH);
```

```
digitalWrite(m12,LOW);
digitalWrite(m21,HIGH);
digitalWrite(m22,LOW);
}

void backward()
{
digitalWrite(m11, LOW);
digitalWrite(m12,HIGH);
digitalWrite(m21,LOW);
digitalWrite(m22,HIGH);
}

void right()
{
digitalWrite(m11, HIGH);
digitalWrite(m12,LOW);
digitalWrite(m21,LOW);
digitalWrite(m22,LOW);
}

void left()
{
digitalWrite(m11, LOW);
digitalWrite(m12,LOW);
digitalWrite(m21,HIGH);
```

```
  digitalWrite(m22,LOW);
}
void Stop()
{
  digitalWrite(m11, LOW);
  digitalWrite(m12,LOW);
  digitalWrite(m21,LOW);
  digitalWrite(m22,LOW);
}
void setup()
{
  // Set console baud rate
  Serial.begin(9600);
  delay(10);
  // Set ESP8266 baud rate
  // 9600 is recommended for Software Serial
  EspSerial.begin(9600);
  delay(10);

  Blynk.begin(auth, wifi, "username", "password"); // wifi
username and password
  pinMode(m11, OUTPUT);
  pinMode(m12, OUTPUT);
  pinMode(m21, OUTPUT);
```

```
  pinMode(m22, OUTPUT);
}

BLYNK_WRITE(V1)
{
 int x = param[0].asInt();
 int y = param[1].asInt();
 // Do something with x and y
/* Serial.print("X = ");
 Serial.print(x);
 Serial.print("; Y = ");
 Serial.println(y);*/
 if(y>220)
 forward();
 else if(y<35)
 backward();
 else if(x>220)
 right();
 else if(x<35)
 left();
 else
 Stop();
}
void loop()
{
```

```
Blynk.run();
}
```

7.Interfacing a PCF8591 ADC/DAC Module with Arduino

Simple to computerized change is a significant errand in installed hardware, as the large majority of the sensors give yield as simple qualities and to nourish them into microcontroller which just comprehend double qualities, we need to change over them into Digital qualities. So to have the option to process the simple information, microcontrollers need Analog to Digital Converter.

Some microcontroller has inbuilt ADC like Arduino, MSP430, PIC16F877A yet some microcontroller don't have it like 8051, Raspberry Pi and so forth and we need to utilize some outer Analog to computerized converter ICs like

ADC0804, ADC0808. Underneath you can discover different instances of ADC with various microcontrollers:

1. How to Use ADC in Arduino Uno?

2. Raspberry Pi ADC Tutorial

3. Interfacing ADC0808 with 8051 Microcontroller

4. 0-25V Digital Voltmeter utilizing AVR Microcontroller

5. Instructions to utilize ADC in STM32F103C8

6. Instructions to utilize ADC in MSP430G2

7. Instructions to utilize ADC in ARM7 LPC2148

8. Utilizing ADC Module of PIC Microcontroller with MPLAB and XC8

In this instructional exercise, we are going to check how to interface PCF8591 ADC/DAC module with Arduino.

Required Components

1. Jumper Cables
2. PCF8591 ADC Module
3. Arduino UNO
4. 100K Pot

PCF8591 ADC/DAC Module

PCF8591 is a 8 piece simple to advanced or 8 piece computerized to simple converter module meaning each stick can peruse simple qualities up to 256. It likewise has LDR and thermistor circuit given on the board. This module has four simple information and one simple yield. It chips away at I2C correspondence, so there are SCL and SDA pins for sequential clock and sequential information address. It requires 2.5-6V supply voltage and have low remain by current. We can likewise control the information voltage by modifying the handle of potentiometer on the module. There are likewise three jumpers on the board. J4 is associated with select the thermistor access circuit, J5 is associated with select the LDR/photograph resistor access circuit and J6 is associated with select the customizable voltage access circuit. To get to these circuits you need to utilize the addresses of these jumpers: 0x50 for J6, 0x60 for J5 and 0x70 for J4. There are two LEDs on board D1 and D2-D1 demonstrates the yield voltage power and D2 demonstrates the force of supply voltage. Higher the yield or supply voltage, higher the power of LED D1 or D2. You can likewise test these LEDs by utilizing a potentiometer on VCC or on AOUT stick.

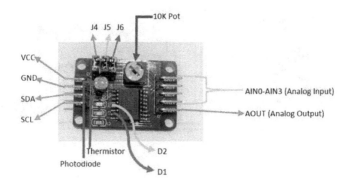

Interfacing PCF8591 ADC/DAC Module with Arduino

Interfacing of PCF8591 with Arduino is exceptionally simple. In this interfacing model, we will peruse the simple qualities from any of the simple sticks and change those qualities by a 100K pot. Initially, associate VCC and GND to 5V and GND of Arduino. Next, interface the SDA and SCL to A4 and A5 of Arduino. Presently, interface a 100K pot with AIN0 as appeared in figure. For LCD, information pins (D4-D7) are associated with computerized pins D5-D2 of Arduino and RS and EN pins are associated with D12 and D11 of Arduino. V0 of LCD is associated with pot and a 100k pot, which is utilized to control the brilliance of LCD.

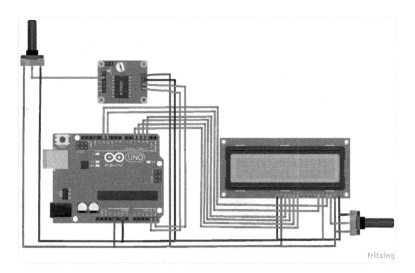

Programming for Arduino PCF8591 **Analog to Digital Conversion (ADC)**

Right off the bat, we have to characterize the library for I2C correspondence and LCD show.

```
#include<Wire.h>

#include <LiquidCrystal.h>
```

At that point characterize a few macros. The primary large scale is for characterizing the location of information transport for IC and second full scale is for characterizing the location of first info stick of module, where the contribution from pot is given.

```
#define PCF8591 (0x90 >> 1)

#define AIn0 0x00
```

Next characterize the stick associations of LCD with Arduino and introduce the worth which we are getting at simple stick.

```
const int rs = 12, en = 11, d4 = 5, d5 = 4, d6 = 3, d7 = 2;

LiquidCrystal lcd(rs, en, d4, d5, d6, d7);

int Value = 0;
```

Presently, how about we come to arrangement work. Here, in first line we've instated the I2C correspondence. Also, in the subsequent line, we've introduced the LCD show on which we are printing the simple qualities. Get familiar with interfacing 16x2 LCD with Arduino here.

```
void setup()

{

Wire.begin();

lcd.begin(16,2);

}
```

In circle work, the principal line is to start the transmission, for example it begins the PCF8591. The subsequent line advises the IC to make the simple estimation at the primary simple information stick. Third line parts of the bargains fourth line gets the deliberate information from simple stick.

```
void loop()

{

Wire.beginTransmission(PCF8591);

Wire.write(AIn0);
```

```
Wire.endTransmission();

Wire.requestFrom(PCF8591, 1);
```

In next segment, put the worth read from simple stick to Value variable characterized before. Also, in next lines, print that incentive to the LCD.

```
Value=Wire.read();

lcd.print("ADC Value=");

lcd.print(Value);

delay(500);

lcd.clear();}
```

At long last transfer the code in Arduino and run it. The simple qualities will begin appearing on LCD show. Modify the pot's handle, and you will see the progressive change in the qualities.

Code

```
#include <LiquidCrystal.h>
#include<Wire.h>
#define PCF8591 (0x90 >> 1)
#define AIN0 0x00
const int rs = 12, en = 11, d4 = 5, d5 = 4, d6 = 3, d7 = 2;
LiquidCrystal lcd(rs, en, d4, d5, d6, d7);
int Value = 0;

void setup()
{
  Wire.begin();
  lcd.begin(16,2);
```

```
}
void loop()
{
  Wire.beginTransmission(PCF8591);
  Wire.write(AIN0);
  Wire.endTransmission();
  Wire.requestFrom(PCF8591, 1);

  Value = Wire.read();
  lcd.print("ADC Value=");
  lcd.print(Value);
  delay(500);
  lcd.clear();
}
```

8.Charlieplexing Arduino - Controlling 12 LEDs with 4 GPIO Pins

Charlieplexing is the process of controlling numerous LEDs utilizing a couple of I/O pins. Charlieplexing is same as multiplexing, yet it utilizes the tri-state rationale (high, low contribution) to lessen the quantity of pins significantly and to pick up effectiveness over multiplexing. The Charlieplexing system is named after its designer, Charlie Allen, who imagined the method in 1995. We recently utilized multiplexing procedure in Arduino to interface 4-digit 7-section show and driving 8x8 LED network.

Charlieplexing enables you to control N * (N − 1) LEDs, where N is the no of pins. For instance, you can control 12 LEDs utilizing 4 Arduino pins 4*(4-1) =12. LEDs are diodes, and in diodes, current streams in just a single course. So in Charlieplexing, we interface two LEDs in parallel with one another however with inverse extremity so just one LED turn on at once. With regards to Arduino or other microcontroller sheets, you never have enough input/yield pins. In the event that you are chipping away at a venture in which you have to interface LCD show, a lot of LEDs, and a few sensors, at that point you are as of now out of pins. In that circumstance, you can charlieplex LEDs to diminish the quantity of pins.

In this instructional exercise, we are going to utilize the Charlieplexing system to control the 12 LEDs utilizing 4 Arduino pins.

Components Required

1. Arduino UNO
2. LED (12)
3. 4 Resistor (330 ohms)

4. Jumper Wires

5. Breadboard

Circuit Diagram

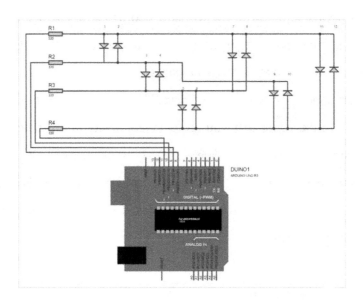

Fundamentally, in this circuit chart, 12 LEDs are associated with 4 Arduino sticks through resistors. Each stick of Arduino is associated with three LEDs. There are six gatherings of LEDs, and in each gathering, 2 LEDs are associated, and the two LEDs are parallel with one another yet with inverse extremity so just one LED turn on at once. So as indicated by the circuit outline to turn on drove 1, there should be a HIGH signal on stick An and a LOW signal on stick B, and stick C and D should be detached. A similar system will be pursued for different LEDs. The full table of stick settings for each LED are given underneath:

LED	Pin 8	Pin 9	Pin 10	Pin 11
1	HIGH	LOW	INPUT	INPUT
2	LOW	HIGH	INPUT	INPUT
3	INPUT	HIGH	LOW	INPUT
4	INPUT	LOW	HIGH	INPUT
5	INPUT	INPUT	HIGH	LOW
6	INPUT	INPUT	LOW	HIGH
7	HIGH	INPUT	LOW	INPUT
8	LOW	INPUT	HIGH	INPUT
9	INPUT	HIGH	INPUT	LOW

10	INPUT	LOW	INPUT	HIGH
11	HIGH	INPUT	INPUT	LOW
12	LOW	INPUT	INPUT	HIGH

After the associations my equipment resembles the picture underneath. As should be obvious from picture there are six gatherings of LEDs and in each gathering 2 LEDs are associated inverse to one another. The Arduino UNO module is fueled by USB port.

Code Explanation

Complete code is given toward the part of the arrangement, here we are disclosing the total program to comprehend the working of the venture.

In the beginning of Arduino code characterize all the stick at which LEDs are associated. From that point onward, characterize the complete number of LEDs and drove state.

```
#define A 8

#define B 9

#define C 10

#define D 11

#define PIN_CONFIG 0

#define PIN_STATE 1

#define LED_Num 12
```

Presently make a network for turning on and off LEDs in a grouping, you can change the arrangement by changing the stick state and stick setup. As per this lattice, LED1 will be turned on first then LED2, etc.

```
int matrix[LED_No.][2][4] = {

//      PIN_CONFIG              PIN_STATE

//      A     B     C     D         A
B    C     D

{ { OUTPUT, OUTPUT, INPUT, INPUT }, { HIGH, LOW, LOW, LOW } },

{ { OUTPUT, OUTPUT, INPUT, INPUT }, { LOW, HIGH, LOW, LOW } },

{ { INPUT, OUTPUT, OUTPUT, INPUT }, { LOW, HIGH, LOW, LOW } },

.................................

.................................
```

Presently inside the void circle, the program will execute the LED_COUNT grid to turn on and off LEDs in the given arrangement.

```
void loop() {

  for( int l = 0; l < LED_Num; l++ ) {

    lightOn( l );

    delay( 1000 / LED_Num );

  }
```

Presently interface the Arduino with the workstation and pick the board and port effectively and after that snap the Upload catch. In case of transferring the code, your LEDs should begin flickering.

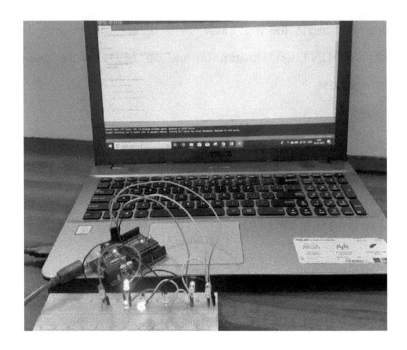

So this is the manner by which Charlieplexing strategy can be used to control numerous LEDs utilizing less Arduino pins. You can utilize this technique to control increasingly number of LEDs. For instance, on the off chance you have to control 20 LEDs, simply alter the network and include the conditions for outstanding LEDs.

Locate the total code beneath.

Code

```c
#define A 8
#define B 9
#define C 10
#define D 11
#define PIN_CONFIG 0
#define PIN_STATE 1
#define LED_Num 12
int matrix[LED_Num][2][4] = {
//      PIN_CONFIG          PIN_STATE
// A    B    C    D    A    B    C    D
{ { OUTPUT, OUTPUT, INPUT, INPUT }, { HIGH,
LOW, LOW, LOW } },
{ { OUTPUT, OUTPUT, INPUT, INPUT }, { LOW,
HIGH, LOW, LOW } },
{ { INPUT, OUTPUT, OUTPUT, INPUT }, { LOW,
HIGH, LOW, LOW } },
{ { INPUT, OUTPUT, OUTPUT, INPUT }, { LOW,
LOW, HIGH, LOW } },
{ { OUTPUT, INPUT, OUTPUT, INPUT }, { HIGH,
LOW, LOW, LOW } },
{ { OUTPUT, INPUT, OUTPUT, INPUT }, { LOW,
LOW, HIGH, LOW } },
{ { OUTPUT, INPUT, INPUT, OUTPUT }, { HIGH,
LOW, LOW, LOW } },
```

```
 { { OUTPUT, INPUT, INPUT, OUTPUT }, { LOW,
LOW, LOW, HIGH } },
 { { INPUT, OUTPUT, INPUT, OUTPUT }, { LOW,
HIGH, LOW, LOW } },
 { { INPUT, OUTPUT, INPUT, OUTPUT }, { LOW,
LOW, LOW, HIGH } },
 { { INPUT, INPUT, OUTPUT, OUTPUT }, { LOW,
LOW, HIGH, LOW } },
 { { INPUT, INPUT, OUTPUT, OUTPUT }, { LOW,
LOW, LOW, HIGH } }
};

void lightOn( int led ) {
 pinMode( A, matrix[led][PIN_CONFIG][0] );
 pinMode( B, matrix[led][PIN_CONFIG][1] );
 pinMode( C, matrix[led][PIN_CONFIG][2] );
 pinMode( D, matrix[led][PIN_CONFIG][3] );
 digitalWrite( A, matrix[led][PIN_STATE][0] );
 digitalWrite( B, matrix[led][PIN_STATE][1] );
 digitalWrite( C, matrix[led][PIN_STATE][2] );
 digitalWrite( D, matrix[led][PIN_STATE][3] );
}
void setup() {}
void loop() {
 for( int l = 0; l < LED_Num; l++ ) {
```

```
    lightOn( 1 );
    delay( 1000 / LED_Num );
  }
}
```

9. Wireless RF Communication using nRF24L01 Module

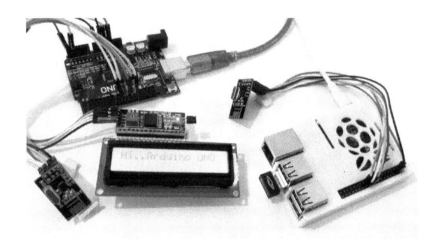

Fashioners utilize numerous remote correspondence frameworks like Bluetooth Low Energy (BLE 4.0), Zigbee, ESP8266 Wi-Fi Modules, 433MHz RF Modules, Lora, nRF and so forth. Furthermore, the determination of medium relies upon the kind of use it is being utilized in. Among every one of the, one well known remote mode for nearby organize correspondence is the nRF24L01. These modules work on 2.4GHz (ISM band) with baud rate from 250Kbps to 2Mbps which is lawful in numerous nations and can be utilized in modern and therapeutic applications. It is likewise asserted that with appropriate reception apparatuses these modules can transmit and get signals upto a separation of 100 meters between them. We recently utilized nRF24L01 with Arduino to control servo engine and make a Chat Room.

Here we will utilize nRF24L01 – 2.4GHz RF Transceiver module with Arduino UNO and Raspberry Pi to set up a remote correspondence between them. The Raspberry pi will go about as a transmitter as well as Arduino Uno will tune in to Raspberry Pi as well as print the message sent by Raspberry Pi utilizing nRF24L01 on a 16x2 LCD. nRF24L01 additionally have inbuilt BLE capacities and it can likewise impart remotely utilizing BLE.

The instructional exercise is isolated into two segments. The principal segment will incorporate the interfacing of nRF24L01 with Arduino to go about as Receiver and the subsequent area will incorporate the interfacing of nRF24L01 with Raspberry Pi to go about as Transmitter.

The nRF24L01 RF Module

The nRF24L01 modules are handset modules, which means every module can send as well as get information however they are half-duplex they can moreover send or get information at once. The module has the nonexclusive nRF24L01 IC from Nordic semi-conductors which is in charge of transmission and gathering of information. The IC imparts utilizing the SPI convention and subsequently can be effectively interfaced with any microcontrollers. It gets much simpler with Arduino since the libraries are promptly accessible. The pinouts of a standard nRF24L01 module is demonstrated as follows

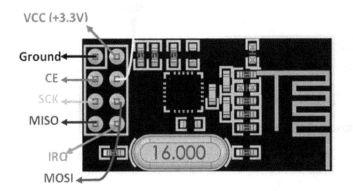

The module has working voltage from 1.9V to 3.6V (ordinarily 3.3V) and devours less present of just 12mA during ordinary activity which makes it battery effective and thus can even keep running on coin cells. Inspite the working voltage is 3.3V the vast majority of the pins are 5V tolerant and thus can be straightforwardly interfaced with 5V microcontrollers like Arduino. Another preferred position of utilizing these modules is that, every module has 6 Pipelines. Which means, every module can speak with 6 different modules to transmit or get information. This makes the module reasonable for making star or work arranges in IoT applications. Additionally they have a wide address scope of 125 one of a kind ID's, henceforth in a shut zone we can utilize 125 of these modules without meddling with one another.

Circuit Diagram

nRF24L01 with Arduino:

The circuit chart for associating nRF24L01 with Arduino is simple as well as doesn't have much segments. The nRF24l01 will be associated by SPI interface as well as the

16x2 LCD is interfaced with I2C convention which uses just two wires.

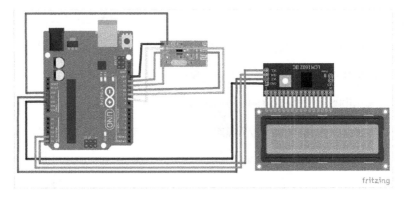

nRF24L01 with Raspberry Pi:

The circuit outline for associating nRF24L01 with Raspberry Pi is additionally basic and just the SPI interface is utilized to associate Raspberry Pi and nRF24l01.

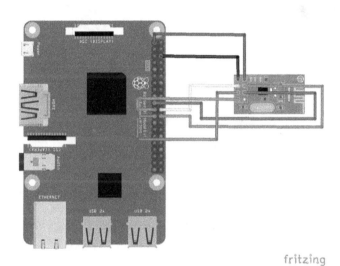

fritzing

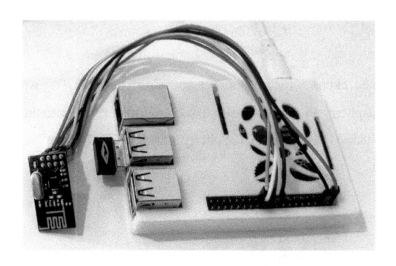

Programming Raspberry Pi to Send Message using nRF24l01

Programming of the Raspberry Pi will be finished utilizing Python3. You can use C/C++ as Arduino. Be that as it may, there is now a library accessible for nRF24l01 in python which can be installed from github page. Note that the python program and the library ought to be on a similar envelope or the python program won't almost certainly discover the library. Subsequent to downloading the library simply concentrate and make an envelope where all projects and library records will be stores. At the point when library establishment is done, simply begin composing the program. The program begin with the incorporation of libraries which will be utilized in code like import GPIO library for getting to the Raspberry Pi GPIOs and import time for getting to the time related capacities. On the off chance that you are new to Raspberry Pi, at that point fall back to beginning with Raspberry pi.

```
import RPi.GPIO as GPIO

import time

import spidev

from lib_nrf24 import NRF24
```

Fix the GPIO mode in "Broadcom SOC channel". This implies you are alluding the pins by the "Broadcom SOC channel" number, these are the numbers after "GPIO"(for example GPIO01,GPIO02...). These are not the Board Numbers.

```
GPIO.setmode(GPIO.BCM)
```

Next we will set it up the pipe address. This location is significant so as to speak with the Arduino collector. The location will be in the hex code.

```
pipes = [[0xE0, 0xE0, 0xF1, 0xF1, 0xE0], [0xF1, 0xF1, 0xF0, 0xF0, 0xE0]]
```

Start the radio utilizing GPIO08 as CE as well as GPIO25 as CSN pins.

```
radio.begin(0, 25)
```

Set payload size as 32 piece, channel address as 76, information pace of 1 mbps and power levels as least.

```
radio.setPayloadSize(32)

radio.setChannel(0x76)

radio.setDataRate(NRF24.BR_1MBPS)
```

```
radio.setPALevel(NRF24.PA_MIN)
```

Open the funnels to begin composing the information and print the fundamental subtleties of nRF24l01.

```
radio.openWritingPipe(pipes[0])

radio.printDetails()
```

Set up a message in the string structure. This message will be sent to Arduino UNO.

```
sendMessage = list("Hi..Arduino  UNO")

while len(sendMessage) < 32:

    sendMessage.append(0)
```

Begin keeping in touch with the radio and continue composing the total string till the radio is accessible. Alongside it, note down the time and print a troubleshoot articulation of message conveyance.

```
while True:

    start = time.time()

    radio.write(sendMessage)

    print("Sent the message: {}".format(sendMessage))
send

    radio.startListening()
```

On the off chance that the string is finished and pipe is shut, at that point print an investigate message of planned out.

```
while not radio.available(0):

    time.sleep(1/100)

    if time.time() - start > 2:

        print("Timed out.")  # print error message if rad
io disconnected or not functioning anymore
```

```
break
```

Quit tuning in to the radio and close the correspondence and restart the correspondence following 3 seconds to send another message.

```
radio.stopListening()     # close radio

    time.sleep(3)  # give delay of 3 seconds
```

The Raspberry program is easy to comprehend in case that you know the nuts and bolts of python. Complete Python program is given toward the part of the bargain.

Executing the Python Program in Raspberry Pi:

Executing the program is simple subsequent to following the underneath steps:

- Spare the Python Program and Library documents in a similar envelope.

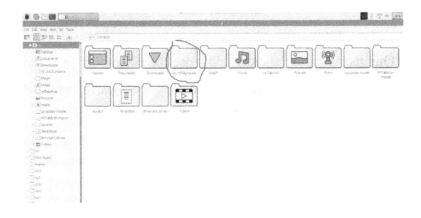

- My program document name for Sender is nrfsend.py and furthermore every records are in a similar envelope

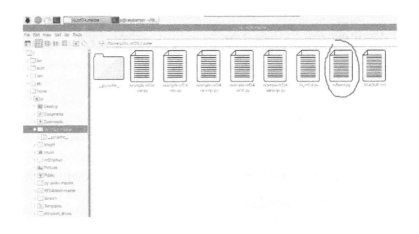

- Go to Command Terminal of Raspberry Pi. What's more, find the python program document by utilizing "disc" order.

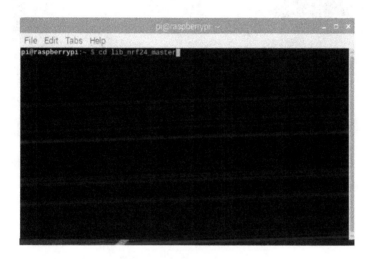

- At that point open the envelope and compose direction "sudo python3 your_program.py" and hit enter. You will most likely observe the fundamental subtleties of nRf24 and the radio will begin sending the messages after like clockwork. The message troubleshoot will show subsequent to sending is finished with all characters sent.

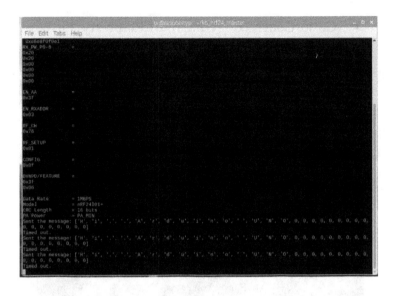

Presently we will consider the to be program as recipient in the Arduino UNO.

Programming Arduino UNO to Receive Message using nRF24l01

Programming the Arduino UNO is like programming the Raspberry Pi. We will pursue comparative techniques however with various programming language and steps. The means will incorporate the perusing some portion of nRF24l01. The library for nRF24l01 for Arduino can be installed from github page. Begin with including important libraries. We are utilizing 16x2 LCD utilizing I2C Shield so incorporate Wire.h library and furthermore the nRF24l01 is interfaced with SPI so incorporate SPI library.

```
#include<SPI.h>

#include <Wire.h>
```

Incorporate RF24 and LCD library for getting to the RF24 and LCD capacities.

```
#include<RF24.h>

#include <LiquidCrystal_I2C.h>
```

The LCD address for I2C is 27 and it is a 16x2 LCD so compose this into the capacity.

```
LiquidCrystal_I2C lcd(0x27, 16, 2);
```

The RF24 is associated with standard SPI sticks alongside CE in stick 9 and CSN in stick 10.

```
RF24 radio(9, 10) ;
```

Begin the radio, set the power level and set channel to 76. Likewise set the pipe address same as Raspberry Pi and open the pipe to peruse.

```
radio.begin();

radio.setPALevel(RF24_PA_MAX) ;

radio.setChannel(0x76) ;

const uint64_t pipe = 0xE0E0F1F1E0LL ;

radio.openReadingPipe(1, pipe) ;
```

Start the I2C correspondence as well as initialise the LCD show.

```
Wire.begin();

lcd.begin();

lcd.home();

lcd.print("Ready to Receive");
```

Begin tuning in to the radio for approaching messages and set the message length as 32 bytes.

```
radio.startListening() ;

char receivedMessage[32] = {0}
```

In case that radio is appended, at that point begin perusing the message and spare it. Print the message to sequential screen and furthermore print to the showcase until the following message arrives. Stop the radio to tune in and retry after some interim. Here it is 10 small scale seconds.

```
if (radio.available()) {
```

```
radio.read(receivedMessage, sizeof(receivedMessage))
;    Serial.println(receivedMessage) ;

Serial.println("Turning off the radio.") ;

radio.stopListening() ;

String stringMessage(receivedMessage) ;

lcd.clear();

delay(1000);

lcd.print(stringMessage);

}
```

Transfer the total code given toward the conclusion to the Arduino UNO as well as trust that the message will be gotten.

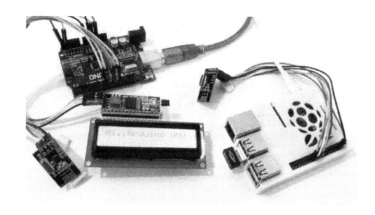

This completes the total instructional exercise on communicating something specific utilizing Raspberry Pi and nRf24l01 and accepting it utilizing Arduino UNO as well as nRF24l01. The message will be printed to the 16x2 LCD. The pipe locations are significant in both Arduino UNO and Raspberry Pi.

Code

NRF Transmitter Side Code (Raspberry Pi):

```
import RPi.GPIO as GPIO  # import gpio
import time      #import time library
import spidev
from lib_nrf24 import NRF24   #import NRF24 library
GPIO.setmode(GPIO.BCM)       # set the gpio mode
```

```python
# set the pipe address. this address shoeld be entered on the
receiver alo
pipes = [[0xE0, 0xE0, 0xF1, 0xF1, 0xE0], [0xF1, 0xF1,
0xF0, 0xF0, 0xE0]]
radio = NRF24(GPIO, spidev.SpiDev())    # use the gpio
pins
radio.begin(0, 25)  # start the radio and set the ce,csn pin
ce= GPIO08, csn= GPIO25
radio.setPayloadSize(32)   #set the payload size as 32 bytes
radio.setChannel(0x76)  # set the channel as 76 hex
radio.setDataRate(NRF24.BR_1MBPS)    # set radio data
rate
radio.setPALevel(NRF24.PA_MIN)  # set PA level
radio.setAutoAck(True)       # set acknowledgement as true
radio.enableDynamicPayloads()
radio.enableAckPayload()
radio.openWritingPipe(pipes[0])     # open the defined pipe
for writing
radio.printDetails()      # print basic detals of radio
sendMessage = list("Hi..Arduino UNO") #the message to
be sent
while len(sendMessage) < 32:
    sendMessage.append(0)
```

```python
while True:
    start = time.time()      #start the time for checking delivery time
    radio.write(sendMessage)   # just write the message to radio
    print("Sent the message: {}".format(sendMessage))   # print a message after succesfull send
    radio.startListening()      # Start listening the radio

    while not radio.available(0):
        time.sleep(1/100)
        if time.time() - start > 2:
            print("Timed out.")  # print errror message if radio disconnected or not functioning anymore
            break
    radio.stopListening()      # close radio
    time.sleep(3)  # give delay of 3 seconds
# >
```

NRF Receiver Side Code (Arduino):

```cpp
#include<SPI.h>              // spi library for connecting nrf
#include <Wire.h>                  // i2c libary fro 16x2 lcd display
```

```cpp
#include<RF24.h>                    // nrf library
#include <LiquidCrystal_I2C.h>      // 16x2 lcd display
library

LiquidCrystal_I2C lcd(0x27, 16, 2);      // i2c address is
0x27

RF24 radio(9, 10) ; // ce, csn pins
void setup(void) {
  while (!Serial) ;
  Serial.begin(9600) ;    // start serial monitor baud rate
  Serial.println("Starting.. Setting Up.. Radio on..") ; //
debug message
  radio.begin();       // start radio at ce csn pin 9 and 10
  radio.setPALevel(RF24_PA_MAX) ;  // set power level
  radio.setChannel(0x76) ;         // set chanel at 76
  const uint64_t pipe = 0xE0E0F1F1E0LL ;   // pipe
address same as sender i.e. raspberry pi
  radio.openReadingPipe(1, pipe) ;       // start reading pipe
  radio.enableDynamicPayloads() ;
  radio.powerUp() ;
  Wire.begin();            //start i2c address
  lcd.begin();             // start lcd
  lcd.home();
  lcd.print("Ready to Receive");  // print starting message
on lcd
```

```
  delay(2000);
  lcd.clear();
}
void loop(void) {
radio.startListening() ;      // start listening forever
  char receivedMessage[32] = {0} ; // set incmng message
for 32 bytes
  if (radio.available()) {      // check if message is coming
    radio.read(receivedMessage,
sizeof(receivedMessage));    // read the message and save
    Serial.println(receivedMessage) ;  // print message on
serial monitor
    Serial.println("Turning off the radio.") ;  // print
message on serial monitor
    radio.stopListening() ;  // stop listening radio
    String stringMessage(receivedMessage) ;  // change
char to string
    lcd.clear();  // clear screen for new message
    delay(1000);  // delay of 1 second
    lcd.print(stringMessage);  // print received mesage
  }
  delay(10);
}
```

10.DIY Arduino Power Supply Shield with 3.3v, 5v and 12v Output Options

Arduino Power Supply Shield

When creating electronic ventures, the power supply is the most significant piece of entire task and there is constantly need of numerous yield voltage power supply. This is on the grounds that various sensors need diverse information voltage and current to run effectively. In this situation, a power supply which can yield different voltages turns out to be significant. There are alternatives that a specialist can use for outside power supply like RPS (managed power supply) or AC connectors however then numerous power supplies will be required and the entire framework will wind up massive.

So today we will plan a Multipurpose Power Supply. The Power Supply will be an Arduino UNO Power Supply Shield which will yield different voltage range, for example, 3.3V, 5V as well as 12V. The Shield will be a run of the mill

Arduino UNO shield with all pins of Arduino UNO can be utilized alongside additional pins for 3.3V, 5V, 12V and GND. Here the PCB is structured on the EasyEDA PCB Designer and made by PCBGoGo.

Likewise check our past DIY Arduino Shields:

1. DIY Arduino Motor Driver Shield

2. DIY Arduino Relay Driver Shield

3. DIY Arduino Wi-Fi Shield

4. DIY LED VU Meter as Arduino Shield

Components Required

1. LM317 – 1 Unit
2. LM7805 – 1 Unit
3. LED(Any Color) – 1 Unit
4. 12V DC Barrel Jack – Unit
5. 220O Resistor – 1 Unit
6. 560O Resistor – 2 Units
7. 1uF Capacitor – 2 Units

8. Burg Pins(20 mm) - 52 Units

9. 0.1uF Capacitor – 1 Unit

Circuit Diagram

The circuit graph and schematic for Arduino Power Supply Shield is quite straightforward and doesn't contain much segment situation. We will utilize 12V DC Barrel Jack for fundamental voltage contribution for the entire Arduino UNO Shield. The LM7805 will change over 12V to 5V yield, comparatively the LM317 will change over 12V to 3.3V yield. LM317 is mainstream Voltage controller IC can be utilized to construct variable voltage controller circuit.

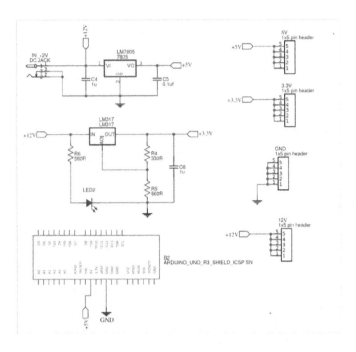

To change over the 12V to 3.3V we are utilizing 330? and 560? as voltage divider circuit. It is essential to put a yield capacitor between the yield of LM7805 and Ground. Thus between the LM317 and Ground. Remember that all grounds ought to be normal and the required track width ought to be picked relying on the present coursing through the circuit.

Fabricating the PCB for Arduino Power Supply Shield

In the wake of preparing the circuit, it's an ideal opportunity to proceed with planning our PCB utilizing the PCB structure programming. As expressed before we are utilizing EasyEDA PCB Designer, so we simply need to change over the schematic to a PCB Board. When you convert the schematic into board, you likewise have to put the segments in the spots as per the plan. Subsequent to changing over the schematic above to board my PCB looked like beneath.

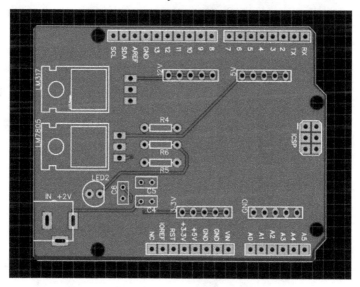

You can download the Gerber record from this connection and send it to the PCBGOGO maker on the web or you can modify the board format as indicated by your hand craft and application.

Ordering the PCB from PCBGoGo

Presently when the total plan is prepared the time has come to get them created. To complete the PCB is very simple, basically pursue the means underneath

Stage 1: Get into www.pcbgogo.com, join if this is your first time. At that point, in the PCB Prototype tab enter the components of your PCB, the quantity of layers and the quantity of PCB you require. Expecting the PCB is 80cm×80cm you can set the measurements as demonstrated as follows.

Stage 2: Proceed by tapping on the Quote Now catch. You will be taken to a page where to set couple of extra parameters whenever required like the material utilized track dispersing and so on. In any case, generally the default esteems will work fine. The main thing that we need to consider here is the cost and time. As should be obvious the Build Time is just 2-3 days as well as it just costs $5 for our PSB. You would then be able to choose a favored dispatching strategy dependent on your necessity.

Stage 3: The last advance is to transfer the Gerber record and continue with the installment. To ensure the procedure is smooth PCBGOGO confirms if your Gerber document is legitimate before continuing with the installment. Along these lines you can sure that your PCB is manufacture well disposed and will contact you as submitted.

Assembling the PCB

After the board was requested, it contacted me after certain days however messenger in a conveniently marked well-pressed box and like consistently the nature of the PCB was wonderful.

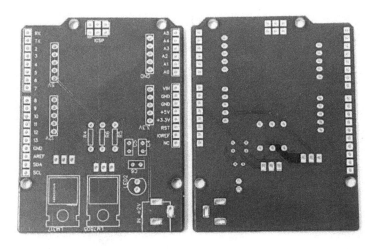

Get the fastening pack and begin putting every one of the parts in the correct stack of the PCB Board. The welding is difficult to complete as there isn't much parts utilized in this venture.

At the point when the binding is done your board should look like beneath.

In this Power Shield the burg pins utilized is of male to male 20 mm connectors. You can utilize Male to Female Burg pins relying on the accessibility. The 20mm burg pins are appropriate for Arduino Shield as well as fits well for on Arduino UNO.

Testing the Power Supply Arduino Shield

It is extremely simple to test the Arduino shield. Simply place the shield on to the Arduino UNO as well as give it a 12V supply from the info barrel jack. The shield can take input voltage of most extreme up to 34V without harming the segments.

You can check all the yield voltage for example 3.3V, 5V and 12V utilizing an advanced multimeter. On the off chance that all went great including planning and welding of the parts, at that point you will almost certainly note down the definite yield voltage at the yield pins.

This completes the total instructional exercise on making an Arduino Uno Power Supply Shield.

www.ingramcontent.com/pod-product-compliance
Lightning Source LLC
Chambersburg PA
CBHW071119050326
40690CB00008B/1276